STATE OF NITA

v.

JAMES WYATT

STATE OF NITA
v.
JAMES WYATT

David S. Rudolf

Thomas K. Maher

Attorneys at Law
Chapel Hill, North Carolina

NATIONAL INSTITUTE FOR TRIAL ADVOCACY

Copies of these materials are available from the National Institute for Trial Advocacy. Please direct inquiries to:

Publications Department
National Institute for Trial Advocacy
Notre Dame Law School
Notre Dame, Indiana 46556
(800) 225-6482
FAX (219) 282-1263

Rudolf, David S. and Thomas K. Maher, *State of Nita v. James Wyatt*, Case File (NITA, 1995).

ISBN 1-55681-476-3

7/96

STATE OF NITA v. JAMES WYATT

CONTENTS

INTRODUCTION

On the evening of Monday, April 5, YR-2, the University of Nita City basketball team played Darrow University for the NCAA championship. It was an overcast, rainy night in Nita City, and the Nita police were concerned about controlling any post-game street celebrations. Ten years earlier, when U.N.C. won their first NCAA basketball championship, students had lit bonfires in the streets, overturned a few cars, and smashed several storefronts on Franklin Street.

James Wyatt, the District Manager of four local Pizza Pub franchise restaurants, was on duty on April 5, YR-2 in the Franklin Street restaurant. Just before the game ended at about 11:25 p.m., Wyatt received a call from another Pizza Pub restaurant requesting his presence there. He told the Franklin Street restaurant manager, Joe Cheshire, that he was going to the other restaurant and then home. Wyatt left the Pizza Pub just after Earl "Little Pearl" Williams hit the winning shot for U.N.C. at the buzzer. Wyatt got into his car and drove a few blocks before U.N.C. students, streaming into the street, made it impossible for him to go on. Wyatt parked his car and returned to the Franklin Street Pizza Pub.

One of the people celebrating U.N.C.'s win was Gary Gilbert, who dropped out of U.N.C. in YR-6 and worked as the assistant manager in a local sporting goods store chain. Gilbert was with a friend, Fran Leving, and watched the game at the Nita Burg and Brew. Right after Little Pearl hit the three pointer to win the game for U.N.C., Gilbert and his friend left the Burg and Brew with the rest of the crowd, heading towards the celebration on Franklin Street. He never made it. Just after leaving the Burg and Brew, while walking down Church Street, Gilbert was struck by a white Miata convertible. He suffered a closed head injury and was in a coma for several days. He has no memory of that evening.

On Friday, April 23, YR-2, following an investigation, the police arrested James Wyatt and charged him with Reckless Driving and Felony Hit and Run. In September, YR-2, Gilbert sued Wyatt and Pizza Pub for damages resulting from the accident.

The applicable law is contained in the statutes and the proposed jury instructions set forth at the end of the file.

All years in these materials are stated in the following form:

YR-0 indicates the actual year in which the case is being tried (i.e., the present year);
YR-1 indicates the next preceding year (please use the actual year);
YR-2 indicates the second preceding year (please use the actual year), etc.

SPECIAL INSTRUCTIONS FOR USE AS A FULL TRIAL

When the case file is used for a full criminal trial, the following witnesses may be called by the parties:

Prosecution:	Fran Leving (This role must be played by a female)
	Det. Paul (Paula) Burns
	Tom (Teresa) Mecklow
Defendant:	James Wyatt (This role must be played by a male)
	Joe (Judy) Cheshire
	Wade (Wendy) Smith

STATE OF NITA

COUNTY OF DARROW

IN THE GENERAL COURT OF JUSTICE
SUPERIOR COURT DIVISION

THE STATE OF NITA,	)
	)
Plaintiff,	)
	)
v.	)
	)
JAMES WYATT,	)
	)
Defendant.	)
	)

INDICTMENT

The Grand Jury, in and for the County of Darrow, State of Nita, upon their oath and in the name and by the authority of the State of Nita, does hereby charge the following offenses under the Criminal Code of the State of Nita.

COUNT I:

That on April 5, YR-2, at and within the County of Darrow, City of Nita, **JAMES WYATT** committed the crime of

HIT AND RUN WITH PERSONAL INJURY

in violation of §20-166 of the Code of Nita in that he did wilfully leave the scene of an accident, when he knew or reasonably should have known that the vehicle he was operating was involved in an accident and that the accident resulted in injury or death to another person.

Contrary to the laws of the State of Nita and against the peace and dignity of the People of the State of Nita.

COUNT II:

That on April 5, YR-2, at and within the County of Darrow, City of Nita, **JAMES WYATT** committed the crime of

RECKLESS DRIVING

in violation of §20-140(a) and (b), in that he drove a vehicle upon a public vehicular area without due caution and circumspection and at a speed or in a manner so as to endanger or be likely to endanger any person.

Contrary to the laws of the State of Nita and against the peace and dignity of the People of the State of Nita.

_____
GRAND JURY FOREPERSON

STIPULATIONS

The following Stipulations have been entered into between the parties:

1. The championship game between U.N.C. and Darrow University ended at 11:22 p.m. on April 5, YR-2.

2. Gary Gilbert suffered a broken leg and a closed head injury on the night of the game. He was in a coma for several days and has no memory of the evening of April 5, YR-2.

3. All statements made by the Defendant, James Wyatt, to the police on April 23, YR-2 were voluntary and in compliance with *Miranda*.

4. Cars registered in Florida have license plates in both the front and the rear.

5. The articles from the *Nita Morning Globe* are true and accurate copies of the articles that appeared in the newspaper on the dates indicated.

DMV-349 (Rev. 7/93)

2 No. of Units Involved	THIS REPORT IS FOR THE USE OF THE DIVISION OF MOTOR VEHICLES. THE DATA IS COLLECTED FOR STATISTICAL ANALYSIS AND SUBSEQUENT HIGHWAY SAFETY PROGRAMMING. DETERMINATIONS OF "FAULT" ARE THE RESPONSIBILITY OF INSURERS OR OF THE STATE'S COURTS.

☐ Supplemental Report

DMV REPORT #

Date			Day of Week	County	Time	Local Use / Patrol Area	Date Received by DMV
04	05	YR-2	MONDAY	NITA	2327	10119/#1	
MONTH	DAY	YEAR			(24 Hour Clock)		

LOCATION

Collision occurred ☒ In ☐ Near TOWN OF NITA CITY   or ___.___ Miles ☐☐☐☐ outside municipal.
Municipality   N S E W

on CHURCH STREET   (R.R.Crossing # ____) __.__ Miles 153.4 ft. ☒☐☐☐
Highway Number, or Highway, Street, (if ramp or service road, indicate on line)   (0 ft.-Intersection) N S E W

from W. FRANKLIN ST. ☐☐☐☐ toward W. ROSEMARY ST.
Use Highway Number, Street Name or Adjacent County or State Line N S E W   Use Highway Number, Street Name or Adjacent County or State Line

☐ VEHICLE 1 .. ☒ HIT & RUN	☐ VEHICLE 2 ☒ PEDESTRIAN ☒ HIT & RUN ☐ OTHER
Driver 1 UNK	Driver 2 GARY GILBERT
Address UNK	Address 2302 ORIOLE DRIVE
City UNK State ___ Zip ___	City NITA CITY State NITA Zip 27707
Same Address on Driver's ☐Yes ☐No Driver's Phone No. W(—)	Same Address on Driver's ☐Yes ☐No Driver's Phone No. W( )
License? H(—)	License? H(919) 555-1262
D.L.# UNK State ___ DOB ___	D.L.# ___ State ___ DOB 9-9-YR-2
Vision — Physical — 3. Intoxication — Restrictions —	Vision 1 Physical 8 3. Intoxication 4 Restrictions —
1. Obstruction 2. Condition	1. Obstruction 2. Condition
Owner UNK	Owner ___
Address UNK	Address ___
City UNK State UNK Zip UNK	City ___ State ___ Zip ___
VIN UNK	VIN ___
Plate # UNK State UNK Year UNK	Plate # ___ State ___ Year ___
Veh. Year UNK Veh. Make MIATA Veh. Type Code P	Veh. Year ___ Veh. Make ___ Veh. Type Code ___
Commercial Vehicle ☐ Yes ☒ No Trailer Type Code —	Commercial Vehicle ☐ Yes ☐ No Trailer Type Code —
Air Bag ☐ Yes ☐ No 1st Trailer No. of Axles —	Air Bag ☐ Yes ☐ No 1st Trailer No. of Axles ___
Deployed ☐ Yes ☐ No Width — inches	Deployed ☐ Yes ☐ No Width — inches
Vehicle Drivable ☒ Yes ☐ No Length — feet	Vehicle Drivable ☐ Yes ☐ No Length — feet
Post Crash Fire ☐ Yes ☒ No 2nd Trailer No. of Axles —	Post Crash Fire ☐ Yes ☐ No 2nd Trailer No. of Axles ___
Rollover ☐ Yes ☒ No Width — inches	Rollover ☐ Yes ☐ No Width — inches
Hazardous Cargo ☐ Yes ☒ No Length — feet	Hazardous Cargo ☐ Yes ☐ No Length — feet
Spilled ☐ Yes ☐ No TAD UNK	Spilled ☐ Yes ☐ No TAD —
Crossed Median ☐ Yes ☒ No Est. Damage $ UNK	Crossed Median ☐ Yes ☐ No Est. Damage $ ___
Removed to UNK	Removed to ___
By DRIVER Authority DRIVER	By ___ Authority —

Other Property Damaged NA	Estimated Damage $ NA	Owner Name NA
		Address NA

OCCUPANT SECTION INSTRUCTIONS: Give Injury Class, Belt/Helmet Usage, Race/Sex and Age of all occupants in the space corresponding to the seat occupied (see codes at top). Names and addresses are necessary for all occupants.

Seat	4. Inj. Class	S. Belt /Hel.	Race /Sex	Age	First Name	Injured Names and Addresses Last Name	Seat	4. Inj. Class	S. Belt /Hel.	Race /Sex	Age	First Name	Injured Names and Addresses Last Name
Left Front	0	9	W/m	40		DRIVER 1	Left Front	A	1	W/m	26	~~████~~ PEDESTRIAN, ~~████~~
Center Front							Center Front						
Right Front							Right Front						
Left Rear							Left Rear						
Center Rear							Center Rear						
Right Rear							Right Rear						

Total Number Occupants 1	Total Number Injured 0	Total Number Occupants	Total Number Injured

Ambulance Requested ☒ Yes ☐ No If yes, Ambulance Arrived At 2337 (24 Hour Clock)

Injured Taken To UNC HOSPITAL ER, NITA CITY, NITA
(Treatment Facility and City or Town)

(left margin, rotated) N.C. COLLISION REPORT FORM — Send To: N. C. Division of Motor Vehicles Raleigh, N. C. 27697-0001

(left margin) MARKS > • < ADDED BY _____ (initial)

POINTS OF INITIAL CONTACT (Write in Codes)		
	VEH. 1	VEH. 2
	26	NA

Passenger Cars/Small Trucks

0. No Contact 25. Rollover
UNDERNEATH: 22 Front 23 Center 24 Rear 26 Unknown

Tractor-Trailers

Motorcycle, Bicycle or Moped

ACCIDENT SEQUENCE	Veh. 1	Veh. 2 or Ped.		Veh. 1	Veh. 2 or Ped.	ROADWAY INFORMATION (See Front)		
6. Veh. Maneuver/Ped. Action	4	18				11. Locality	3	19. Road Defects	7
7. First Harmful Event		6	Speed Limit (for each vehicle)	25	—	12. Development Type	4	20. Road Condition	2
7. Most Harmful Event	6	6	Estimated Original Traveling Speed	15	—	13. Road Feature	14	21. Light Condition	4
8. Object Struck	4	1	Estimated Speed at Impact	15	—	14. Road Character	1	22. Weather	3
9. Distance to Object Struck	1	8	Tire Impressions Before Impact (ft.)	0	—	15. Road Class	5	23. Traffic Control	11
10. Vehicle Defects	7	8	Distance Traveled After Impact (ft.)	0	—	15. Number of Lanes	3	Operating ☐ Yes ☐ No
						17. Road Configuration	2	Visible ☐ Yes ☐ No
						18. Road Surface	3	

INDICATE NORTH

PARKING LOT AREA

DRY CLEANERS

W. FRANKLIN ST

W. ROSEMARY ST.

RED

← 153.4 → ← 161.8 →

NITA MUNICIPAL PARKING LOT AREA

Vehicle 1 was Traveling ☒N ☐S ☐E ☐W on   Vehicle 2 was Traveling ☐N ☐S ☐E ☐W on

DESCRIBE WHAT HAPPENED: VEHICLE #1 WAS TRAVELING NORTH ON CHURCH STREET, AFTER TURNING OFF OF W. FRANKLIN STREET. VEHICLE #1 STRUCK A PEDESTRIAN CROSSING/WALKING ACROSS CHURCH STREET TOWARD W. FRANKLIN STREET. VEHICLE #1 LEFT the SCENE OF THE ACCIDENT BEFORE OFFICERS ARRIVED. VEHICLE #1 COULD NOT BE LOCATED. SEE ALSO DESCRIPTION OF INVESTIGATION, attached.

CIRCUMSTANCES CONTRIBUTING TO THE COLLISION (Check as many as apply)				RESERVED FOR CITY OR OTHER USE
DRIVER 1 2	DRIVER 1 2	DRIVER 1 2		
☐ ☐ 1. None	☐ ☐ 10. Pass stopped school bus	☐ ☐ 19. Safe movement violation		
☐ ☐ 2. Alcohol use	☐ ☐ 11. Passing on hill	☐ ☐ 20. Following too closely	RESERVED FOR STATE USE	
☐ ☐ 3. Drug use	☐ ☐ 12. Passing on curve	☐ ☐ 21. Improper backing		Driver 1	Driver 2
☐ ☐ 4. Yield	☐ ☐ 13. Other improper passing	☐ ☐ 22. Improper parking	24. Direction		
☐ ☐ 5. Stop sign	☐ ☐ 14. Improper lane change	☐ ☐ 23. Unable to determine	25. Violation		
☐ ☐ 6. Traffic signal	☐ ☐ 15. Use of improper lane	☐ ☐ 24. Left of center	26. Misc. Action		
☐ ☐ 7. Exceeding speed limit	☐ ☐ 16. Improper turn	☐ ☐ 25. Right turn on red	27. Charges		
☒ ☐ 8. Exceeding safe speed	☐ ☐ 17. Improper or no signal	☒ ☐ 26. Other Hit + Run Personal Injury	28. Investigating Agency		
☒ ☐ 9. Failure to reduce speed	☐ ☐ 18. Improper vehicle equipment			

WIT-NESSES: Name FRAN LEVING   Address 644 Jones Ferry Road   Phone No. 919 555-3178
Name ___   Address Nita City, NITA   Phone ( )

ARRESTS: Name ___   Charge(s) ___
Name ___   Charge(s) ___

Sign Here DET. PAUL BURNS   3205   NITA City Police Dept   4-5-YR-2
Officer's Rank and Name   Number   Department   Date of Report

DMV-349 FORM—ACCIDENT SEQUENCE CODES

1. VISION OBSTRUCTION
1. None
2. Vehicle window(s) obscured
3. Trees, crops, brush, etc.
4. Building(s)
5. Embankment
6. Sign(s)
7. Hillcrest
8. Parked vehicle(s)
9. Moving vehicle(s)
10. Blinded, headlight
11. Blinded, sunlight
12. Blinded, other lights
13. Other (write in narrative)
14. Unknown

2. PHYSICAL CONDITION
1. Normal
2. Ill
3. Fatigued
4. Asleep
5. Impairment due to medicine, alcohol or drugs
6. Other physical Impairment

3. INTOXICATION
1. Had not been drinking
2. Drinking—test given
3. Drinking—test refused
4. Unknown
5. Drinking—no test

4. INJURY CLASS
- K—Killed
- A—Incapacitating
- B—Nonincapacitating
- C—No visible—But Complaint of pain
- O—No injury

5. Belt/Helmet
1. None or not used
2. Lap only
3. Lap and shoulder
4. Child restraint system
7. If motorcycle, Helmet in use

6. VEHICLE MANEUVER/ PEDESTRIAN ACTION: VEHICLE
1. Stopped in travel lane
2. Parked out of travel lanes
3. Parked in travel lanes
4. Going straight ahead
5. Changing lanes or merging
6. Passing
7. Making right turn
8. Making left turn
9. Making U turn
10. Backing
11. Slowing or stopping
12. Starting in roadway
13. Parking
14. Leaving parked position
15. Avoiding object in road
16. Other (describe)

PEDESTRIAN
17. Crossing at Intersection
18. Crossing not at Intersection
19. Coming from behind parked vehicle
20. Walking with traffic
21. Walking against traffic
22. Getting on or off vehicle
23. Standing in road
24. Working in road
25. Playing in road
26. Lying in road
27. Other in road
28. Not in road

7. FIRST/MOST HARMFUL EVENT: RAN OFF ROAD
1. Right
2. Left
3. Straight ahead

NON-COLLISION
4. Overturn
5. Other

COLLISION OF MOTOR VEHICLE WITH PEDESTRIAN
6. Pedestrian
7. Parked vehicle
8. Train
9. Bicycle
10. Moped
11. Animal
12. Fixed object
13. Other object

COLLISION OF MOTOR VEHICLE WITH ANOTHER MOTOR VEHICLE
14. Rear end, slow or stop
15. Rear end, turn
16. Left turn, same roadway
17. Left turn, different roadways
18. Right turn, same roadway
19. Right turn, different roadways
20. Head on
21. Sideswipe
22. Angle
23. Backing

8. OBJECT STRUCK (excluding another motor vehicle in traffic)
1. None
2. Parked vehicle
3. Bicycle, moped
4. Pedestrian
5. Animal
6. Tree
7. Utility pole (with or without light)
8. Luminaire pole (Non-breakaway)
9. Luminaire pole (breakaway)
10. Official highway sign (non-breakaway)
11. Official highway sign (breakaway)
12. Commercial sign
13. Guardrail end on shoulder
14. Guardrail face on shoulder
15. Guardrail end in median
16. Guardrail face in median
17. Shoulder barrier end } Non-Guardrail
18. Shoulder barrier face } Guardrail

9. DISTANCE TO OBJECT STRUCK
1. In road
2. Right of road, 0-10 ft.
3. Right of road, 11-30 ft.
4. Right of road, over 30 ft.
5. Left of road, 0-10 ft.
6. Left of road, 11-30 ft.
7. Left of road, over 30 ft.
8. None or N/A
9. Straight ahead, 0-10 ft.
10. Straight ahead, 11-30 ft.
11. Straight ahead, over 30 ft.

10. VEHICLE DEFECTS
1. Defective brakes
2. Defective headlights
3. Defective rear lights
4. Defective steering
5. Defective tires
6. Other defects
7. Not known if defective
8. No defects detected

19. Median barrier end } Non-Guardrail
20. Median barrier face } Guardrail
21. Bridge rail end
22. Bridge rail face
23. Overhead part of underpass
24. Pier on shoulder of underpass
25. Pier in median of underpass
26. Abutment (supporting wall of overpass)
27. Curb, median or traffic island
28. Catch basin or culvert on shoulder
29. Catch basin or culvert in median
30. Ditch bank
31. Mailbox
32. Fence or fence post
33. Construction barrier
34. Crash cushion
35. Other object (write in narrative)

11. LOCALITY
1. Rural (<30% developed)
2. Mixed (30% to 70% developed)
3. Urban (>70% developed)

12. PREDOMINANT DEVELOPMENT TYPE
1. Farms, woods, pastures
2. Residential
3. Commercial
4. Institutional
5. Industrial

13. ROAD FEATURE
1. Bridge
2. Underpass
3. Driveway, public
4. Driveway, private
5. Alley intersection
6. Intersection of roadways
7. Non-Intersection median crossing
8. End or beginning of divided highway
9. Interchange ramp
10. Interchange service road
11. Railroad crossing
12. Tunnel
13. Other (write in narrative)
14. No special feature

14. ROAD CHARACTER
1. Straight, level
2. Straight, hillcrest
3. Straight, grade
4. Straight, bottom
5. Curve, level
6. Curve, hillcrest
7. Curve, grade
8. Curve, bottom

15. ROAD CLASS
1. Interstate
2. U. S. route
3. N. C. route
4. State secondary route
5. Local street
6. Public vehicular area
7. Private road, property or driveway

16. NUMBER OF LANES
Enter "0" if parking lot

17. ROAD CONFIGURATION
1. Undivided, one-way
2. Undivided, two-way
3. Divided

18. ROAD SURFACE
2. Grooved concrete
3. Smooth asphalt
4. Coarse asphalt
5. Gravel
6. Sand
7. Soil
8. Other (write in narrative)

19. ROAD DEFECTS
1. Loose material on surface
2. Holes, deep ruts
3. Low shoulders
4. Soft shoulders
5. Other defects
6. Under construction with defects
7. No defects
8. Under construction no defects

20. ROAD CONDITION
1. Dry
2. Wet
3. Muddy
4. Snowy
5. Icy
6. Other (write in narrative)

21. LIGHT CONDITION
1. Daylight
2. Dusk
3. Dawn
4. Darkness (street lighted)
5. Darkness (street not lighted)

22. WEATHER
1. Clear
2. Cloudy
3. Raining
4. Snowing
5. Fog, smog, smoke, dust
6. Sleet or hail

23. TRAFFIC CONTROL
1. Stop sign
2. Yield sign
3. Stop and go signal
4. Flashing signal with stop sign
5. Flashing signal without stop sign
6. RR gate and flasher
7. RR flasher
8. RR crossbucks only
9. Human control
10. Other (write in narrative)
11. No control present

INITIAL REPORT

CASE NO: 10119-YR-2

VICTIM(S) NAME(S):   Gary Gilbert

DETECTIVE: Paul Burns

DATE: April 6, YR-2

DESCRIPTION OF INVESTIGATION:

On the evening of April 5, YR-2, I was on special duty at the Post Office downtown because of the NCAA championship game. At about 11:27 p.m., we got a call on the radio that there appeared to be a serious accident on Church Street, and that it might be a hit and run. Because all uniformed officers were assigned to crowd control and I was downtown anyway, I was asked to go to the scene.

I got to Church Street at about 11:32 p.m., and saw a uniformed officer there with the victim and a girl in her early twenties, who was crying. I asked whether she was the driver of the car, and she didn't respond at first. The uniformed officer told me that she was a friend of the victim, and was with him when he was hit. The victim was lying in the road about halfway between Rosemary and Franklin Streets. He was horizontally across the street with his head near the east curb on Church Street and his feet towards the west.

There were a number of people in the area, some of whom saw the victim on the ground after the accident. All of them were intoxicated, and none remembered seeing the impact. I could not find anyone who actually saw the accident except for the girl who was with the victim. She told me that the rest of the people who were there at the time the victim was hit left to go to the celebration on Franklin Street. She did not know their names.

The ambulance arrived at 11:34 p.m., and left the scene with the victim, who was identified as Gary Gilbert, about 10 minutes later. Once the ambulance left, I attempted to talk with the girl, who identified herself as Fran Leving.

Ms. Leving was still crying and very upset, and couldn't give me many details. She did say that the car was a white Miata, that the license plate was not from Nita because it had orange numbers, and that the plate number was YEA-330. She kept saying "It's weird -- Little Pearl's number is 33 and Gary was yelling about his shot just before he got hit." She told me the car was probably going around 15 m.p.h. when she saw it on Church. She didn't know how fast it was going when it hit the victim. She said she heard a loud bang, turned and saw the victim lying on the ground, not moving. Then she broke down and couldn't talk any more.

I proceeded to take the measurements I needed, and to fill out the DMV report. I then looked around the parking lots on Church Street, to see if there was any car matching the description I had been given. Although the lots were two-thirds full, there was no white Miata. I left the area of the accident at about 12:15 a.m.

SUPPLEMENTAL REPORT

CASE NO:	**10119-YR-2**
VICTIM(S) NAME(S):	**Gary Gilbert**
DETECTIVE:	**Paul Burns**
DATE:	**April 6, YR-2**
RE:	**Telephone Call from Tom Mecklow**

This afternoon at about 1:35 p.m. I received a telephone call from a man who identified himself as Tom Mecklow. Mr. Mecklow told me that he had read the story about Gary Gilbert in the *Nita Morning Globe*, and believed he had some information that was important.

Mecklow said that he was the owner of Mecklow's Jewelers, which is located on West Franklin near Mallette Street in Nita City, and that he had operated his store there for the past 11 years, first with his father (who owned the store since YR-24) and then by himself. Mecklow said that he had watched the game on TV last night, and decided to walk downtown when the score was tied with about 10 minutes to go. Mecklow told me that his store's front door was smashed by some drunk college kids the last time U.N.C. won the championship, and he was worried it might happen again if U.N.C. won.

Mecklow lives on North Columbia, a few blocks from Franklin Street. Mecklow decided to walk to his store, even though it was raining, because he did not want to bring his car downtown in the middle of a victory celebration. He walked up Columbia towards Franklin. He went into the Nita Sports Bar to get a beer and watch the end of the game. The bar was crowded and very noisy. When Darrow University was ahead by 5 points with approximately 50 seconds to go, he decided he should head to his store as the students in the bar were getting pretty rowdy.

After Mecklow left the bar, he walked along the north side of West Franklin, heading west. He was walking quickly, as it was raining hard and there were already a few students in the streets. It took a few minutes for him to get to Church Street. As he got there, he heard a car engine behind him. He turned and saw a small car coming west on Franklin. He noticed it was a light colored sports car, and it made a right turn onto Church. He is not sure of the speed, but thought it was going too fast as there were already a few, scattered students running across the street. It was the only car he saw driving on that stretch of Franklin as he walked to his store. He is not sure what type of sports car it is, but is pretty sure it must have been the car mentioned in the newspaper.

I asked Mr. Mecklow if he would be willing to come by the police station to give me a written statement. He said he would stop by on his way home from work this evening.

STATEMENT OF TOM MECKLOW
(Handwritten)

My name is Tom Mecklow and I own Mecklow's Jewelers in Nita City. I am writing this statement as requested by Detective Burns.

On the night of the championship game, I stopped by the Nita Sports Bar to have a beer and watch the end of the game. I left just before the game ended, and as I got to Church Street, I saw a small white Miata with a black convertible top coming down West Franklin Street towards me. It was raining hard and the car was going very fast, over 45 m.p.h. It made a sharp right turn onto Church, and I could hear the tires screeching. I think that the driver was white, in his thirties with curly hair, and he may have been wearing glasses. I'm not sure. I noticed the car because it almost hit me when it turned right onto Church. There were no other cars on the street. It was near the time when I heard everyone yelling and screaming that O.N.C. won.

I didn't hear about the accident that night, or I would have called the police sooner. I just stayed in my store while all the drunk students went down to East Franklin Street yelling and screaming, standing on parked cars, and setting bonfires in the middle of the street. Shortly after I got in the store I heard sirens, but did not realize that there had been an accident. I was scared they were going to trash my store, but nothing was damaged. As soon as I read about the accident in the newspaper, I called police. I think the guy I saw in the car is the same guy described in the wanted poster that police have distributed to all the merchants. I apologize for not coming in earlier, but this matter slipped my mind until I read about the victim's family in the newspaper yesterday.

April 18, YR-2   Tom Mecklow

SUPPLEMENTAL REPORT

CASE NO:	**10119-YR-2**
VICTIM(S) NAME(S):	**Gary Gilbert**
DETECTIVE:	**Paul Burns**
DATE:	**April 21, YR-2**
RE:	**Interview with Joe Cheshire**

On April 21, YR-2, I interviewed Joe Cheshire, who is the manager of the Pizza Pub on Franklin Street, about the evening of the NCAA championship game. Mr. Cheshire told me that he remembers the night U.N.C. won the national championship. Mr. Wyatt, his supervisor, was at the restaurant to help keep things under control. Wyatt left about the time the game ended. Cheshire remembers a waitress warned Wyatt that he would never get his car out of Franklin Street once the celebration began. Wyatt was driving a white Miata convertible. Cheshire saw Wyatt a little later that night, when Wyatt came back to the restaurant, and Wyatt did not tell Cheshire that he had been in an accident. He just said he couldn't get his car out. Cheshire said he would be surprised if Wyatt left an accident knowing that somebody was seriously hurt, as he is just not that type of person.

I then asked Cheshire for Wyatt's address, which he gave me. I asked him not to tell Mr. Wyatt about my visit.

SUPPLEMENTAL REPORT

CASE NO: 10119-YR-2

VICTIM(S) NAME(S):   Gary Gilbert

DETECTIVE: Paul Burns

DATE: April 23, YR-2

RE: Arrest and Statement of James Wyatt

On April 21, YR-2, based upon information supplied by Florida law enforcement relating to the license plate on the car which struck Gary Gilbert on April 5, YR-2, I was able to trace the plate to a YR-5 Miata owned by James Wyatt. Further investigation revealed that Wyatt worked for Pizza Pub in Nita City, on October 2, YR-4. I then interviewed the manager of the Franklin Street Pizza Pub in Nita City and confirmed that Mr. Wyatt worked there the night of the championship game.

On April 23, YR-2, after locating the Miata in the parking lot outside Mr. Wyatt's apartment, I went to the apartment and spoke to Mr. Wyatt. I asked him if he would come with me to the Nita City Police Station, which he agreed to do. After he drove his vehicle to the Police Station, Mr. Wyatt was advised of his rights and voluntarily waived them. He then gave us the attached statement and drew his route on the map I provided. Mr. Wyatt was then charged with reckless driving and felony hit and run. He was released on a $1,000.00 bond.

I left the Pizza Pub as the game ended because I got a call that there was a problem at the Estes Drive restaurant. I pulled out of the Pizza Pub driveway and made a right hand turn at the corner of Church Street and Franklin. The streets were full of people and it was raining. I never used my accelerator, I was coasting with my foot on the brake going about 10 m.p.h. Several people ran by me, at me, around me, beat their fists on my trunk. I glanced around, another group of people hit my front hood. I stopped immediately and got out of my car, the people were still streaming by me. I didn't know what to do other than to park my car in the lot to the left. It was still pouring down rain and kids running and screaming about the game. I had no reason to believe I hurt anyone, I thought they were goofing around. I walked back to the Pizza Pub in the rain with thousands of students. It was still pouring down rain. I waited about 20-30 mins. for the streets to clear, but it wasn't looking like it would settle down. I walked back to my car, nothing seemed unusual still thousands of kids running around in the rain. I left in my car. At no time did I seriously think anyone was hurt seriously. I thought everyone was just hyped up about the game.

James Wyatt   4/23/ YR-2

Description of Map prepared by James Wyatt on
April 23, YR-2

1. Point where crowd prevented car from
   continuing down Church Street and I got
   out of my car to decide what to do.

2. Route taken to park my car when I couldn't
   continue down Church Street after the game.

3. Place where I parked my car after trying to
   go down Church Street after the game.

4. Route taken back to Pizza Pub after parking
   my car.

5. Route taken back to my car around 11:40 p.m.

James Wyatt

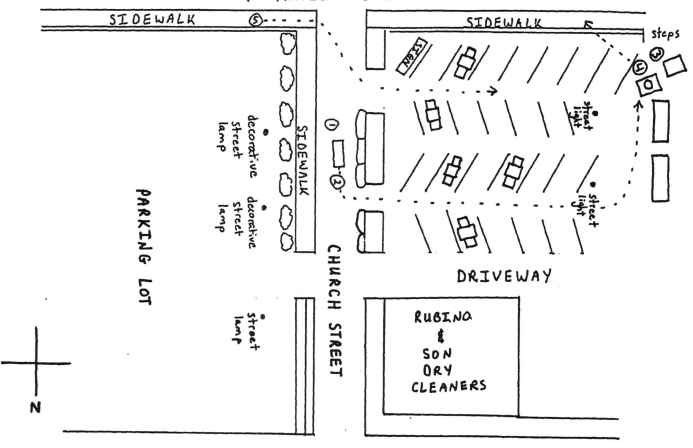

FRANKLIN STREET

SIDEWALK ⑤

SIDEWALK   steps

③

④

SIDEWALK

①

②

street light

street light

decorative street lamp

decorative street lamp

street lamp

PARKING LOT

CHURCH STREET

DRIVEWAY

RUBINO & SON DRY CLEANERS

N

ROSEMARY STREET

SUPPLEMENTAL REPORT

CASE NO: 10119-YR-2

VICTIM(S) NAME(S): Gary Gilbert

DETECTIVE: Paul Burns

DATE: April 26, YR-2

RE: 911 Call by James Wyatt

At the time he was arrested on April 23, James Wyatt claimed that on April 5, YR-2 he called the Nita City Police Department to report that his car had been damaged by students pounding on it. Wyatt stated that he placed this call to 911. When I asked him why he would call 911 to report property damage, Wyatt hesitated for a moment, and then said that he first tried calling the main number for the Nita City Police Department twice, but that it was busy both times.

After receiving this information, I checked the log of complaints taken by the operator at the Nita City Police Department between 10:35 p.m. on April 5, YR-2 and 1:04 a.m. on April 6, YR-2. A copy of that log, which is always kept by the operator on duty, is attached to this supplemental report. However, it should be noted that the police did not respond to all calls on that evening. Rather, only emergency calls were responded to.

I then checked the tapes of the 911 calls made during this same time period. I found a tape of a call made at 11:37 p.m. on April 5, YR-2 by a person who identified himself as James Wyatt. A true and accurate transcript of this tape is also attached to this supplemental report.

NITA CITY POLICE DEPARTMENT

TELEPHONE LOG

(919)-555-2767

TIME PERIOD: April 5, YR-2, 2235 to April 6, YR-2, 0105

Time of Call	Area	Location	Nature of Complaint
2235	1	Henderson	illegally parked vehicle
2245	3	815 S. Elliott	Alarm (business)
2247	1	Henderson	illegally parked vehicle
2253	1	Cameron/Mallett	disabled vehicle
2255	1	7-11	drunk & disruptive
2258	3	NITA Printing	Alarm
2301	1	Henderson	illegally parked vehicle
2301	1	Burg &Brew	assault
2306	4	Sports Bar	escort
2306	1	Miami Subs	drunk & disruptive
2318	1	404 McDade	hang up
2324	1	504 W. Franklin	Vandalism
2326	1	Church/Rosemary	Accident PI
2329	1	411 Church	noise
2324	1	303 McMasters	hang up
2343	1	S. Columbia	Fire alarm
2347	3	NITA Printing	alarm
2358	1	Bus Station	EMS
2359	3	Wendy's	escorts
0000	1	E. Franklin	accident

State v. Wyatt

0004	3	NITA Hotel	Burglary
0010	4	104 Cedar St.	info
0013	3	NITA Printing	alarm
0015	3	120 S. Estes Comm. Ctr.	Alarm
0018	1	523 E. Rosemary	illegally parked vehicle
0028	4	Airport Rd.	Accident PD
0033	1	Franklin St. Mkt.	Alarm
0034	1	The Parlor	Assault
0039	1	Granville Towers	Accident PD
0041	3	E. Franklin	Vandalism
0042	2	Hanes Art Ctr.	EMS
0044	4	Sports Bar	escorts
0051	1	E. Franklin	Assault
0051	3	NITA Printing	alarm
0053	3	Red Roof Inn	Fire alarm
0056	1	Fast Fare	Fight
0059	1	Granville East	EMS
0104	1	McDonalds	man gun/shooting
0105	1	W. Rosemary	B&E Auto

TRANSCRIPT OF 911 CALL

Date of Call: April 5, YR-2
Time of Call: 2337

Operator: 911. May I help you?

Male: Yes. I was just driving down Church Street coming from the Pizza Pub
                   and some students were pounding on my car as I tried to drive down the
                   street, and I don't know if someone ....

Operator: (Interrupting) Where did this happen?

Male: On Church Street in Nita City.

Operator: Sir, could you please just call the Nita City Police Department to report
                   that. The number is 555-2767.

Male: O.K. Have you gotten any other reports ....

Operator: (Interrupting) Sir, we're very busy right now. Please call the police
                   department number.

Male: O.K. Thank you.

SUPPLEMENTAL REPORT

CASE NO:	**10119-YR-2**
VICTIM(S) NAME(S):	**Gary Gilbert**
DETECTIVE:	**Paul Burns**
DATE:	**February 25, YR-1**
RE:	**Investigation of Wyatt's alleged trip to Kansas City**

Within the past month we have received information that James Wyatt claims to have been in Kansas City in the days immediately following the hit and run accident on April 5, YR-2.

As a result, I called Pizza Pubs' corporate headquarters in Kansas City today, and spoke with one of their Vice-Presidents, Wade Smith. Mr. Smith recalled that Mr. Wyatt came to Kansas City sometime last April, but he could not recall the exact dates. He indicated that he would look through the corporate records and fax me whatever information he could find.

Map of Nita City

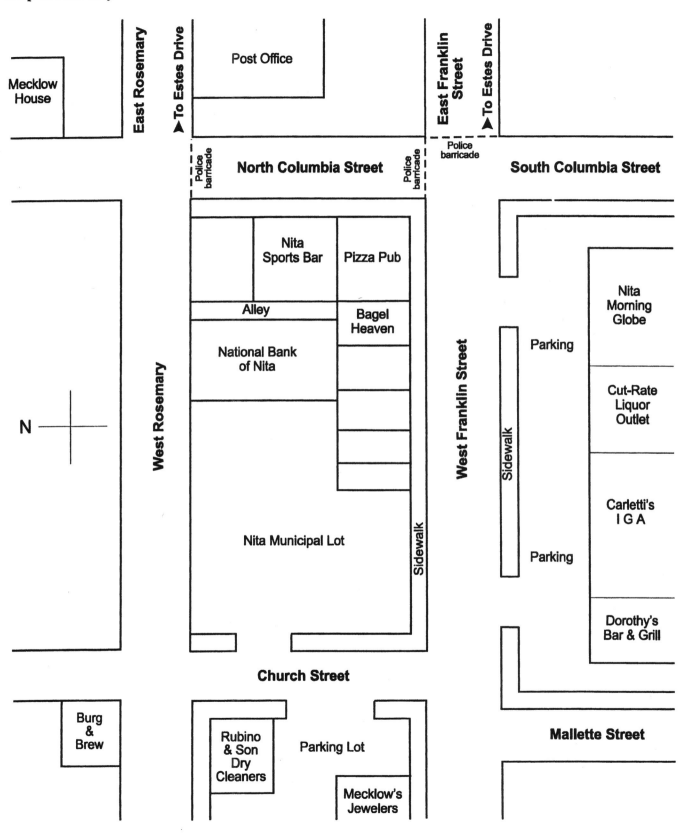

NITA DEPARTMENT OF MOTOR VEHICLES
OFFENSE HISTORY

NAME: James Wyatt

DOB: 1/21/YR-45

D.L.#:   958039

Date of Offense	Location	Charge	Disposition
10/14/YR-4	Evanston, IL	Speeding (87/65)	Plead guilty to speeding (74/65). Fined $100 + costs
12/5/YR-4	Evanston, IL zone)	Speeding (school	Plead not guilty. Found Guilty. Fined $200 + costs
9/18/YR-3	Nita City, Nita	Reckless Driving	Plead guilty to Unsafe Movement. Fined $75 + costs

NITA POLICE DEPARTMENT

OFFENSE HISTORY

NAME: Fran Leving

DOB: 2/19/YR-24

Date of Offense	Location	Charge	Disposition
12/23/YR-5	Nita City, Nita	Worthless Checks (4 counts)	Plead guilty to misdemeanor; Restitution of $350 plus $100 costs

WANTED

NITA CITY POLICE DEPARTMENT
828 Airport Road
Nita City, Nita 27514

Telephone: (919) 555-2767   Crime Stoppers: 1-800-555-7867

NAME: John Doe

ADDRESS: Unknown

COMPLAINT NO.:   10119

RACE: White   SEX: Male

DOB & AGE: 35-40's   HEIGHT: 5/10"

WEIGHT: 160-170   BUILD: medium build

HAIR: Brown   EYES:

COMPLEXION: Clean

ADDITIONAL DESCRIPTION:

Hair short, possibly glasses, clean dressed in button down shirt and slacks.

NCIC#   WANTED FOR: Felonious Hit and Run

DATE OCCURRED: 04/05/YR-2   TIME OCCURRED: 23:25

LOCATION OCCURRED: Church Street near Rosemary

DESCRIPTION OF OFFENSE: Suspect was driving a white Miata convertible,

   possible license YEA-330, unknown state (orange numbers on white background)

   Vehicle came from Franklin Street on Church Street and struck the victim in the street.

   The vehicle might have damage to the hood area.

                   INVESTIGATING OFFICER: Det. P. Burns

Photo -- View down Church Street from West Rosemary to West Franklin

Photo -- View from West Franklin down Church towards Rosemary

POLICE SEEK FLEEING MOTORIST

NITA CITY - Police were searching Tuesday for the driver of a car that struck and seriously injured a pedestrian who was walking downtown toward the U.N.C. victory celebration Monday night.

Police said the driver of a white, late-model sports car struck Gary Gilbert, 26, of Nita City, as Gilbert crossed Church Street just north of West Franklin Street about 11:30 p.m.

The car driver, described as a well-dressed white man in his 30s or 40s with brown hair and glasses, stopped his car after the impact, a police source said.

He stepped out and looked at Gilbert, then returned to his car and drove away, the source said.

Gilbert, who works at Nita Sporting Goods, was listed in serious condition at U.N.C. Hospitals Tuesday.

Anyone with information may telephone Nita City police at 555-2767.

NOTE: This article appeared on the front page of the *Nita Morning Globe*.

FAMILY HOPES, WAITS AFTER HIT-RUN

NITA CITY - In the euphoria following U.N.C.'s championship April 5, Gary Gilbert and a friend hurried from the Burg and Brew restaurant up Church Street toward the celebration on Franklin.

"Gary's a huge U.N.C. fan," said Fran Leving, who had gone with Gilbert to Burg and Brew to see the big game. "He was real excited. We all were. We were just jumping in the street, yelling."

About 11:30 p.m., as Gilbert led fans up Church, a white Miata turned onto the street from West Franklin. Leving said the car did not slow.

"This car just turned into the road and cruised," Leving said. "I don't think he cared about the people in the street."

Within seconds the Miata struck Gilbert, throwing him onto the hood of the Miata, according to Leving. The driver backed up, got out and looked at the body, motionless on the pavement. A U.N.C. student who saw the man said he seemed frightened, shocked. Then the driver got back in his car and drove away.

Nearly two weeks later, Gilbert remains in the hospital he entered the night of the accident. The driver has not been found.

And Gilbert's family is waiting for police to catch the man who struck Gary.

"I'm surprised at the person who did this," Norma Gilbert said. "It was an accident, but it doesn't seem like that anymore."

Nita City Detective Paul Burns said police are waiting too, for a call. Fliers along Franklin Street and on the University of Nita City campus ask those with information on the hit-and-run to call the Crimestoppers number: 1-800-555-7867. Crimestoppers has offered to reward people who help police catch the driver.

The driver faces a felony leaving the scene of an accident charge, which carries a maximum penalty of five years in prison, Burns said. Police are circulating a description of the suspect -- a white man, in his 30s or 40s, who wore glasses and was well-dressed late April 5.

POLICE PRAISED FOR ARREST OF DRIVER

NITA CITY - Family and friends of a man struck by a car during U.N.C.'s NCAA championship celebration hailed the police work that led to the arrest of a Nita City man on felony hit-and-run charges.

But their enthusiasm was tempered by the knowledge that Gary Gilbert remained in a hospital, almost three weeks after the April 5 accident.

Fran Leving, a friend, said she couldn't blot out the memory of that night.

Moments after she and Gilbert rushed from an area bar to join the Franklin Street celebration, a car struck Gilbert and sent him flying through the air.

Gilbert remains in stable condition at U.N.C. Hospital, a hospital spokeswoman said.

Nita City police arrested James Wyatt, 45, late Friday and charged him with hitting Gilbert and speeding from the scene of the Church Street accident before police arrived.

Wyatt, a district manager for Pizza Pub, was released Friday night on a $1,000 secured bond. His first appearance in court is scheduled Monday.

He did not return phone calls Saturday to his house.

Investigators had little information to go on, said Nita City Police Department spokeswoman Jane Cason. The description they got of the car included a partial number from an unspecified out-of-state license plate, a description of the driver who got out of his car to look at Gilbert and a description of the car as a white, late-model Miata convertible.

"It was real vague," she said. "The bulk of information was from witnesses who were there when the accident occurred."

Detective Paul Burns contacted law enforcement agencies around the Southeast and beyond and gave them the partial license and vehicle information, Cason said. "The Florida Highway Patrol came through for us," she said.

With a little creative manipulation of the license plate information, including changing a reported 0 to a D, Florida authorities pointed Nita City police to an Illinois car owner, Cason said. The owner told Burns the car had been sold to a man living in Nita City: Wyatt.

"Detective Burns did a great job in this," Cason said: "It was certainly the negative part of what happened that night. It was a serious crime, and we're just glad to have arrested somebody."

The Gilbert family and friends had posted fliers around Nita City and the U.N.C. campus asking people with information about the accident to contact police.

Leving, who has started a fund to help offset the Gilbert family's medical bills, said the reaction at the hospital to news of the arrest was boisterous.

"We were just overjoyed," the 23 year old waitress said. "We wanted the man caught. The whole floor was like 'Yes!' Everyone was screaming and clapping."

FRAN LEVING

Probable Cause Hearing*

February 12, YR-1

Fran Leving , having been called to testify and being duly sworn, testified as follows:

My name is Fran Leving, and I live at the Old Well Apartments on Jones Ferry Road near Highway 54 in Nita City with my roommate, Sharon Winoski. I am 24 years old, and graduated from U.N.C. in May, YR-3. I am planning on going to graduate school in social work, but need to save up some money first. I have been working for the past two years as a waitperson at the Magnolia House, which is one of the nicer restaurants in Nita City.

I have known Gary Gilbert since I was in college. We met in January, YR-5, when I was a sophomore. We dated for about a year, and then became good friends. He went to U.N.C., but dropped out in YR-6 because his father got sick and he needed to work to help his family. He started working at NSG (Nita Sporting Goods) which is a chain of four or five sporting goods stores in Nita City. That's where I first met him, when I went in to buy some running shoes. He was only a salesperson at that time, but worked his way up to an assistant manager. He also took some classes at U.N.C., and is only a few credits away from being able to graduate.

Gary played basketball in high school and in the Intramural League at U.N.C., and is a big U.N.C. basketball fan. On the day of the NCAA championship game, which was Monday, April 5, YR-2, I called Gary to find out if he wanted to go somewhere to watch the game that night. He agreed to pick me up at my apartment at about 7:30 p.m., so that we could go to the Burg and Brew on West Rosemary and get a good seat.

Gary was a few minutes late, and we didn't get to the Burg and Brew until about 8:00 p.m. I remember that the pre-game show was just starting. I think they were interviewing Dick Vitale, who I think is pretty obnoxious. Anyway, the Burg and Brew was already getting crowded, and Gary and I got two seats near the back of the restaurant.

By the time the game started at 9:00 p.m., the place was packed. There were probably 150 people in a space designed for half that. Everyone was yelling and screaming, and almost everyone was drinking beer. Each time U.N.C. scored, you couldn't ever hear the person next to you. I probably had a couple of beers before the game started, and two or three more during the game. It's hard to say exactly, because the people setting next to us had pitchers, and they would refill my glass from time to time. Gary only had one beer before the game started, because we agreed that he would be the designated driver. I do not think he had anything else to drink that night, except I remember him asking for water because the salsa we were eating was hot. That's all we had for dinner.

---

*The transcript of Leving's testimony has been excerpted so that only the answers are reprinted here. Assume that she was called to testify by the prosecutor, and that this is a true and accurate reproduction of her answers.

The game was incredibly exciting, close the whole way, and people were really pumped up. I think the biggest lead was five points, by Darrow, with a minute left. I thought we were going to lose, but Gary said that a minute was a lifetime in these games, and that our coach was a master in these situations. Gary was right. It seemed like every time Darrow came down we fouled them, they would miss at least one free throw, and we would come back to score. We finally tied the score with about fifteen seconds left. Darrow called time, then scored with about four seconds left. We called time, and then Little Pearl hit the three pointer to win the game at the buzzer. Everyone at the Burg and Brew went crazy! The place cleared out fast. Everyone headed towards East Franklin Street, where the police had barricades to block off the street so everyone could celebrate.

Since Gary and I moved to the front of the restaurant near the end of the game, we were probably in the first group to get out the door. I was pretty excited, and I had a buzz from the beer, but I definitely wasn't drunk. Gary was really excited too.

After we left the Burg and Brew, Gary and I walked down Church Street heading towards Franklin. I'm not sure how many people were on the street, but there were a lot. Probably more than 100. There were too many people for the sidewalk, so Gary and I were walking in the street, right near the east curb. It was chilly and it was drizzling, but everyone was so excited that no one really cared about the weather. People were running around, yelling and shouting "We're Number One", and jumping on each other, but it was all in good fun.

When we were about halfway between Rosemary and Franklin Street, I saw a small white sports car make a right hand turn from Franklin Street onto Church Street, and I remember thinking to myself that the car didn't seem to be slowing down at all, despite all the people on the street. I would estimate the car was going 35-40 m.p.h. when it made the turn. I know it seemed to be travelling really fast to me, considering we were not the only people on the street and it had been raining all day so the road was wet. I got scared and stepped back up on the sidewalk. As I did, I turned and saw Gary get hit on the street. He sort of flipped over the front hood and landed on his head. I didn't hear any brakes, or tires screeching, or horn blowing. The guy just plowed into Gary. He would have hit me too if I hadn't stepped back on the sidewalk when I did.

After he hit Gary, the guy stopped, pulled his car back a few feet, and got out. I saw that he was driving one of those little Miata's. It was a white convertible, and it had one of those telephone antennas on the top of the front windshield. I looked down, saw Gary was lying on the street and wasn't moving, and then I looked back at the driver and started screaming at the guy "call 911." He just stood there by the door of his car, looking at me, then down towards Gary, then back to me. I think he said something like "Where'd he come from?", but I couldn't hear too well because everyone was yelling and I was really scared about Gary. Anyway, the guy didn't do anything, or even try to give Gary any assistance. He just stood there staring. I couldn't see his face too well, because there was a streetlamp directly behind him that I was looking into. However, I could tell that he was a male in his late 30's or early 40's, about 5'10", with brown curly hair. He was wearing nice slacks and a dress shirt, definitely not jeans and a tee shirt. I also distinctly remember that he was wearing glasses. I don't know why, I just remember looking at his glasses. His car was only about ten feet from where Gary was, and about 15 feet from where I was standing on the sidewalk. I also remember his license plate, because it seemed weird at the time. It was YEA - 330. Thirty-three is Little Pearl's number.

Gary was just lying there, and after a few seconds there was a group of people all around him. Other people were just yelling and screaming about the game. I guess they didn't see Gary lying there, or maybe they didn't care. Anyway, I heard someone say that 911 was on the way, so I pushed through the crowd and bent down next to Gary. That's the last I saw of the guy or his car that night.

The ambulance came pretty quickly. I would guess it was about five minutes, but I'm not sure because I was so upset. There weren't any visible wounds and there was no blood, but Gary was moaning, not really conscious. The longer he stayed that way, the more hysterical I became. I remember a police officer talking to me just after the ambulance left. He must have been a Detective because he wasn't wearing a uniform. I have no idea what I said to him, or even whether it made sense. I just wanted to get to the hospital to see how Gary was doing. I do recall that he asked me about the man and his car, and that we looked for it but couldn't find it. The guy just took off and left Gary lying there.

I saw the guy on TV when he was arrested, and I'm pretty sure it was the same guy. I just can't be absolutely positive. I only saw him for 20 or 30 seconds.

1		)	having first been duly
2	**PAUL BURNS,**	)	sworn, was examined
3		)	and testified as follows:

4   **DIRECT EXAMINATION BY MR. FOX:**

5   Q: Would you state your name and employment, please?

6   A: Paul Burns. I am a detective with the Nita City Police

7   Department.

8   Q: Detective Burns, did you investigate a hit and run that

9   occurred on April 5, YR-2 and injured one Gary Gilbert?

10   A: Yes, I did.

11   Q: And when did you become involved in the investigation?

12   A: Very late in the evening on the 5th day of April, YR-2.

13   Q: And did you receive any information from -- as far as did

14   you interview any witnesses initially?

15   A: I spoke to Fran Leving.

16   Q: And did you receive any information from the witness?

17   A: Yes, I did.

18   Q: What was that?

19   A: I learned -- got some information about the accident and a

20   possible license plate number of the suspect vehicle.

21   Q: And what license plate number did you receive?

22   A: YEA-330, she believed it to be Florida. If not Florida,

23   Georgia.

24   Q: Now, what did you do upon receiving this information?

1 A: I was still soliciting information from the public on any

2   kind of additional information -- anybody that might have

3   seen the car or the driver or had gotten a positive license

4   plate number on this car. We knew that there were several

5   witnesses who had left the scene before we got there.

6 Q: And how were you going about soliciting information about

7   that?

8 A: Through television, newspapers, radio, things like that.

9 Q: Did you have any type of composite or information as to the

10   vehicle that you were looking for?

11 A: Yes, we had released a description of the driver and a

12   possible description of the vehicle we were looking for.

13 Q: And what description of the vehicle did you release?

14 A: We were looking for a small, white, late-model sports car

15   with a convertible top, possibly a Miata.

16 Q: And how did you go about publishing this to the public?

17 A: Again, it was through television, newspapers, that type of

18   thing.

19 Q: And did you release any description as to the person who

20   might be the driver of that vehicle?

21 A: Yes, we did.

22 Q: What description was that?

23

24

1 A: A white male in his mid-thirties to mid-forties, brown hair,

2   medium to slight build, possibly glasses, about 5 foot 10

3   inches tall, I believe is what it was.

4 Q: Did you release any information as to the location and when

5   this occurred?

6 A: Yes.

7 Q: What information was that?

8 A: It was generally known that it was a hit-and-run accident

9   that had taken place on Church Street the night of the NCAA

10   final game.

11 Q: Did you, yourself, see any of the notices published about

12   the incident?

13 A: Yes, I saw it in the newspaper in Nita -- <u>Nita Morning</u>

14   <u>Globe</u>. I also saw some posters put up in local stores.

15 Q: Did you see it on any of the television stations as well?

16 A: I did not. But I heard it was on TV from other people.

17 Q: Now, did you attempt to determine the registration -- the

18   owner of this particular vehicle or registration?

19 A: Yes, I did.

20 Q: And how did you go about doing that?

21 A: Through our DCI computer. I initially ran those license

22   plates through Georgia and Florida and neither one of them

23   came back with anybody's vehicle in those states. It was

24   not a valid tag as it was given to me.

1   Q: And then what did you do?

2   A: I contacted Florida Highway Patrol Investigative Division

3   and gave them the information I had asking for any kind of

4   vehicles registered with license plate numbers close to what

5   I was given.

6   Q: And what happened?

7   A: I received a response of four license plate numbers, one of

8   which was YEA-33D Florida.

9   Q: What did you do?

10   A: I checked the ownership information of that vehicle, and

11   found out the vehicle had just been sold recently to James

12   Wyatt.

13   Q: It was YEA-33D?

14   A: That's correct.

15   Q: And the plate registration number you had received was YEA-

16   330?

17   A: That's correct.

18   Q: Once you learned that it had been sold to the defendant,

19   what did you do?

20

21

22

23

24

1   A: I went to Blackwood Mountain Apartments, where the defendant

2   lives, contacted the management, explained to them what I

3   was investigating, that I had information -- I went and

4   looked first of all to see if the vehicle was at this

5   residence, and it was not. So I checked with them to see if

6   Mr. Wyatt was living there in fact and if he had a vehicle

7   matching that description. They indicated he did, and that

8   he matched the description I gave them as to the person

9   involved in this incident.

10 Q: And what did you do at that time?

11 A: I instructed them just if they saw the car again to let me

12   know. They called within, I would say, an hour later,

13   indicated that the vehicle was back on the apartment

14   complex. I had a patrol vehicle go to the apartment

15   building, verify the car was there and just to keep it from

16   leaving if they could until I arrived.

17 Q: And how long did it take you to arrive there?

18 A: Approximately 30, 35 minutes. It was right around 5 o'clock

19   in the afternoon.

20 Q: When you arrived there, what did you do?

21 A: Spoke with Mr. Wyatt, told him who I was, why I was there,

22   explained to him I was investigating a hit-and-run accident

23   that happened the night of the NCAA final game.

24

1 Q: And what did you do after you advised him of what you were

2   looking at?

3 A: He made a short statement to me to the effect of he had been

4   down there that night and saw all the people and they were

5   jumping on his car and beating on his car. He didn't know

6   what was going on. I then asked him to come voluntarily in

7   his vehicle to the Nita City Police Department which he did.

8 Q: Did you look at the vehicle itself?

9 A: Yes, I did.

10 Q: And did it still have the same registration plate on it?

11 A: It did.

12 Q: Was it a Florida or a Georgia plate?

13 A: Florida.

14 Q: And did you see any damage to the car?

15 A: Initially I noticed fairly substantial damage -- there was a

16   noticeable dent on the hood near the front of the car,

17   between the headlights.

18 Q: And did Mr. Wyatt come back with you to the Nita City Police

19   Department?

20 A: He did.

21 Q: And what happened there?

22

23

24

1 A: We sat down. I told him again what I was looking at, why I

2   was talking to him. I advised him of his rights. We -- I

3   told him I needed to talk to him about what had taken place,

4   that I had information from the Pizza Pub restaurant on

5   Franklin Street that he was there the night of the NCAA

6   final game and left sometime around the end of the game. He

7   subsequently gave me a written statement as to what had

8   transpired that night when he left.

9 Q: And do you have a copy of that statement?

10 A: I don't have it in my hands. I have it -- it's in the file

11   I believe.

12 Q: Did you at any time ask him if had seen any of the notices

13   or anything on the television?

14 A: Yes, I did.

15 Q: And what did he say?

16 A: He indicated he works long hours. He doesn't follow the

17   news and doesn't get a newspaper, so he had not heard about

18   it.

19 Q: Did you ask him about the damage to his car?

20 A: Yes, I did.

21 Q: Do you recall what his response was there?

22 A: I believe -- to the best of my recollection he told me that

23   they were -- some people had jumped up on his car and were

24   beating his car with their fists.

1   Q: Did you --

2   A: He also indicated to me when he went back to the Pizza Pub

3   that night he tried to call the police by dialing 911. He

4   said he was told to try the main number, and that he then

5   tried the non-emergency number and couldn't get through,

6   tried twice, but he didn't try since then.

7   Q: Did you make or cause to be made photographs of this car?

8   A: No, I did not.

9   Q: When was it that you first saw the vehicle? What was the

10   date?

11   A: 4/23/YR-2.

12   Q: Can you describe the car?

13   A: Yes. It's a two-door white Miata convertible with --

14   appeared to be two dents, a small one almost in the dead

15   center of the rear trunk and a substantial one on the front

16   hood, between the headlights.

17   Q: Did Mr. Wyatt ever indicate that he called the police --

18   called the other number, not the 911 number, after that

19   evening?

20   A: He just indicated to me he didn't know he had done anything,

21   so he hadn't made any attempts beyond that first night to

22   call us.

23

24

1	Q: Did you ask him why he attempted to call 911 on that
2	particular evening -- call the Nita City Police Department
3	on that occasion?
4	A: I believe he indicated to me that he thought it was unusual
5	a lot of people were out there beating on his car and
6	whatnot, and so that's why he stopped and wanted to call us.
7	Q: Did you contact -- at what point did you contact the
8	official at the Pizza Pub?
9	A: On the 21st, two days before he was arrested -- in the
10	afternoon.
11	Q: Excuse me, was that after you knew that he was employed
12	there?
13	A: That's correct. When I first initially made contact with
14	the owner of the vehicle and he indicated the vehicle had
15	been sold to Mr. Wyatt, I received information that his
16	employment was with Pizza Pub. So suspecting that he may be
17	associated with the one downtown, I went to that location
18	and spoke to them. I believe the gentleman's name I spoke
19	with was Joe Cheshire, a manager at the restaurant.
20	**MR. FOX:** I don't have any further questions for
21	the witness.
22	
23	
24	

CROSS EXAMINATION BY DEFENSE COUNSEL:

Q: Detective, were you on duty the evening -- I think you said you got involved in this case on Monday, the 5th of April?

A: That's correct.

Q: Were you on duty that evening?

A: Yes, I was.

Q: And do you recall what the weather conditions were like out on the street right after the game?

A: No, I do not. I was -- my position was inside the post office building, so I wasn't aware of what the weather was like by personal knowledge.

Q: Have you seen the videotape of the victory celebration I prepared from the news broadcast?

A: Yes, sir, I reviewed it at your request.

Q: And did the tape fairly and accurately depict the scene that night?

A: In general, yes. I don't remember it being quite that bad on Church. It was on East Franklin.

Q: Now, when you first got involved in this, it was the night of the accident.

A: Yes, sir.

1 Q: And I believe you said you got some information from Ms.

2   Leving. Did you make any notes of that -- those

3   conversations?

4 A: Yes, I did.

5 Q: Do you have those in court with you or --

6 A: Again, they're in the file. Basically I can verbalize to

7   you what the essence of the conversation was if that's what

8   you're looking for.

9 Q: Yes, sir.

10 A: I spoke to Ms. Leving. What I was trying to determine is if

11   she got a good look at this individual and was able to put

12   any kind of a description together that would assist me in

13   locating who this person was. She indicated that she didn't

14   believe that she had gotten a good enough look at the

15   individual to positively identify him. She also gave me a

16   general description of the car and the numbers of the

17   license plate. That was about the essence of the

18   conversation at that point.

19 Q: Now, I believe you said that when you got involved in the

20   case you publicized the fact that you were looking for

21   information.

22 A: That's correct.

23 Q: And articles appeared, did they not, in the <u>Nita Morning</u>

24   <u>Globe</u>?

1 A: I believe so. I didn't clip them out or anything.

2 Q: Let me just show you what I've marked as Defendant's Exhibit

3   A for purposes of this hearing and ask you to take a look at

4   it and see if that jogs your memory at all about the

5   article?

6   [THEREUPON, WITNESS EXAMINES DOCUMENT.]

7 A: I may have seen this in the newspaper. I just don't recall.

8   I saw many articles and things.

9 Q: In any event, there were a couple of articles in the day or

10   two after the accident, correct?

11 A: That's correct.

12 Q: And there were newscasts in the day or two after the

13   accident?

14 A: Yes, sir, I believe there were.

15 Q: And when you spoke with Mr. Wyatt you asked him where he was

16   in the week, say, after the accident, didn't you?

17 A: When I first spoke to him, I did not.

18 Q: But later on you did?

19 A: I believe my questioning was confined to the events of that

20   night. I did ask him if he had heard anything about this.

21   He indicated that he had been working long hours, wasn't

22   following the news and didn't read the newspaper.

23 Q: Do you recall him telling you that he was in Kansas City,

24   Missouri the week after this game?

1 A: No, I do not.

2 Q: You didn't jot down any notes about that?

3 A: I don't recall him saying that. I didn't make any note to

4   that effect, no, sir.

5 Q: Now, the -- by the way, on the evening in question do you

6   recall if there were any barricades that the police had sort

7   of set up in anticipation of the potential post-game victory

8   celebration on Franklin Street?

9 A: Not by personal knowledge, no, sir.

10 Q: Well, just from your knowledge as a police officer.

11 A: I believe there were barricades supposedly placed at

12   Franklin and Columbia and barricades placed at Henderson and

13   Franklin due to the fact they anticipated closing the 100

14   block of East Franklin Street. Those are the only

15   barricades that I had any information on.

16 Q: So you don't know about barricades anywhere else or whether

17   they were --

18 A: No, sir.

19 Q: -- or weren't?

20 A: No, sir.

21 Q: Did Ms. Leving indicate where she was when she saw the

22   person who was driving the vehicle?

23

24

1   A: She was walking down Church Street leaving the area of Burg

2   and Brew, and I believe she stated that she had heard the

3   impact but didn't actually see the accident, saw the vehicle

4   stop, saw the driver step out of his car. At that point she

5   indicated to me that she thought the person was going to

6   stay there, so she didn't think anymore about it.

7   Q: Did she say how long she had seen this particular person?

8   A: Just a matter of a few seconds.

9   Q: And up to this point, has any lineup, photographs or

10   otherwise been done for her?

11 A: I showed her a set of six pictures, yes, sir.

12 Q: And was she able to select any of them?

13 A: She selected the picture of Mr. Wyatt but not with one

14   hundred percent certainty.

15 Q: And when was that done roughly?

16 A: I would say probably Tuesday of the week following his

17   arrest.

18 Q: Now, in terms of the damage to the car that you found, I

19   think you said that you found two dents in the car?

20

21

22

23

24

1 A: I initially noticed only one dent on the front hood. It was

2   brought in. We had it towed to our impound lot; and when

3   myself and C. T. Alston, our ID technician, were examining

4   the car closer, we then noticed a smaller dent in the rear

5   trunk. I think Wyatt had told us about that one at the

6   police station.

7 Q: So the second dent was harder to notice than the first?

8 A: That's correct.

9 Q: And the first dent was up in the front --

10 A: Of the hood, correct.

11 Q: How far from the headlights would you say it was? How many

12   inches from where the headlights are?

13 A: Roughly three or four inches, very close.

14 Q: And what about the other dent. Where was that located?

15 A: It was probably six or eight inches below the back of the

16   convertible top. C. T. Alston measured all of those, but I

17   didn't. It was slightly off to one side.

18 Q: Which side was it off to, the driver's side or the

19   passenger?

20 A: The passenger.

21 Q: Any other dents or marks on the car that you and Officer

22   Alston noticed?

23 A: Not that I recall.

24

1	Q:	And I believe that Mr. Wyatt told you -- I think he
2		testified to this -- that people had been beating on his
3		car.
4	A:	That's what he told me, yes.
5	Q:	Was Mr. Wyatt cooperative with you?
6	A:	Yes, he was.
7	Q:	He went down to the station voluntarily.
8	A:	That's correct.
9	Q:	You didn't have to place him under arrest at that point.
10	A:	That's correct.
11	Q:	He drove his car down there initially.
12	A:	That's correct.
13	Q:	He didn't ask to speak to a lawyer or anything like that?
14	A:	No, sir. We -- I read him a statement of his Miranda rights
15		and he signed the waiver.
16	Q:	So he knew he didn't have to talk with you.
17	A:	That's correct.
18	Q:	How long did you interview him for?
19	A:	Approximately 20 minutes -- 20, 25 minutes, somewhere in
20		that range, I would say.
21	Q:	And then at the conclusion of the interview, you asked him
22		to write out a statement.
23	A:	That's correct.
24	Q:	And he did.

1   A: That's correct.

2   Q: He did that voluntarily as well.

3   A: Yes, he did.

4   **DEFENSE COUNSEL:**   That's all I have.   Thank you

5   very much.

JAMES WYATT

Deposition*

January 30, YR-1

1   James Wyatt, having been called to testify and being duly sworn, testifies as follows:
2
3   My name is James Wyatt, and I live on Blackwood Mountain Road, in the county just north
4   of Nita City. I was born on January 21, YR-45, and am a manager for Pizza Pub in the Nita area.
5
6   I grew up in Wisconsin, and went to college at the University of Wisconsin. I graduated
7   with a degree in business in YR-24, but I ended up becoming the track coach at my old high school.
8   I have always enjoyed working with young people, and I enjoyed being the track coach, although it
9   meant teaching social studies as well. I got married in YR-20, and have two children; David, born
10   YR-17, and Susan, born YR-14. Over the years I turned down several opportunities to move to
11   bigger schools, and a local college, because my wife and I enjoyed being in a small town.
12
13   In YR-9 my father-in-law persuaded my wife and I that we should move to Florida, where
14   he lived. We moved down, and I could not find a teaching/coaching job that paid enough to live on,
15   so I went to work in my father-in-law's business. He owned several fast-food franchises, and by YR-
16   6 I was managing several of the franchises. I did not really enjoy the work, or the long hours, but
17   the money was good. The long hours, and my stress level, put a strain on my marriage, and in YR-4
18   we separated. I took a position with Pizza Pub, a fast growing company that runs pizza restaurants
19   nationwide, mostly in college towns. I started off managing a Pizza Pub in Evanston, Illinois.
20   Evanston is a college town near Chicago. In fact, I bought the Miata from another employee while
21   I was living in Evanston. I registered the car in Florida because I still owned a house there and I
22   hoped to get back together with my wife.
23
24   I have two speeding tickets and an unsafe movement conviction. The traffic charges
25   happened the first few months I had the car, and was not familiar with how fast it would go. In YR-3
26   I was offered the chance to come to the Nita area and manage several Pizza Pubs, including two in
27   Nita City, and two more in neighboring Capitol City. My title was District Manager. I was told that
28   if things went well, I would be considered for a promotion to Regional Manager, which involves
29   supervising restaurants in two states, and would mean a large increase in pay. As I have alimony and
30   child support, including two college educations in the next few years, to pay for, I could use the
31   money.
32
33   I moved into an apartment just north of Nita City at the end of the summer of YR-3, and
34   started getting the restaurants ready for the school year. Summers are relatively slow for us, as most
35   of our business comes from college students. I was eager to make a good impression, so I put in a
36   lot of hours, and made detailed reports to Pizza Pub's main office in Kansas City. I knew that there

---

*Wyatt was deposed in connection with a civil suit filed by Gilbert, which is still pending. The transcript of
Wyatt's testimony has been excerpted so that only the answers are reprinted here. Assume that he was called to
testify by the plaintiff, and that this is a true and accurate reproduction of his answers.

1   were several other people who were being considered for the Regional Manager slot, and at my age
2   I was not about to let this fall through. I got a good bunch of kids working at the restaurants, after
3   I weeded out some of the slackers. I spent time each week at each of the restaurants, keeping up with
4   the student managers, and I travelled every month or so to Kansas City for company meetings. The
5   meetings were run by Wade Smith, who had the final say on my promotion.
6
7   Things were going pretty well, and Smith seemed impressed. Profits were up, and I had
8   managed to cut back on the amount of damage and theft and bad checks that the restaurants had been
9   experiencing in the past. By March of YR-2, Smith made it clear that I had a real shot at the
10   promotion. March was pretty hectic because the NCAA tournament got under way. I am not a big
11   basketball fan, and not a fan of the conference in which U.N.C. plays; my heart is still in the
12   Midwest. However, the restaurants were popular places for the kids to watch the games as we serve
13   pitchers of beer and have several televisions. During the tournament several U.N.C. games were
14   televised, either during the afternoon or evening. During the early games the crowds were okay, not
15   too much drunken rowdiness. As U.N.C. got closer to the finals, the students watching the games
16   got rowdier, and I got worried about keeping things under control.
17
18   U.N.C. made it to the final game against Darrow University by winning a game on Saturday,
19   April 3, YR-2. I had the following Sunday and Monday to get ready for the big game on Monday
20   night, plus I had to get ready to leave for Kansas City early Tuesday morning. I was to make a short
21   presentation to Smith and some other executives about some marketing promotions for a new
22   product, and I wanted it to go well. I had heard from some of the people I met in Nita City that
23   U.N.C.'s last national championship lead to complete chaos; students tipping over cars, climbing
24   trees, setting bonfires, and generally taking over the downtown block of Franklin Street. One of our
25   Pizza Pubs is only a block from the main section of Franklin. I knew that it would be packed, and
26   that win or lose there would be chaos after the game. I called the police about arranging for some
27   officers to be in the area, but was told that I was on my own as far as protecting a private restaurant
28   was concerned; they were just too busy with crowd control on the streets. The officer I spoke to did
29   tell me that I should prepare for the worst as there had been problems in several restaurants the last
30   time U.N.C. won; vandalism and kids stealing cases of beer from a local store, stuff like that.
31
32   I decided that I would spend the evening at the Franklin Street restaurant helping out the kids
33   who worked there. The second Pizza Pub is closer to the mall, on Estes Drive about two miles east
34   of campus, and I did not expect it to be as full or as rowdy. I spent Monday getting ready for my trip
35   to Kansas City, and checking on the other restaurants, before going to the Franklin Street Pizza Pub.
36   I got there about 7:00, and was able to park my car in front of the restaurant. There is a semi-circle
37   parking area in front of the restaurant where I park if there is room, so I was not actually on Franklin
38   Street. I met with Joe Cheshire, the manager of the restaurant, and reviewed with him and the wait
39   staff my concerns. We decided to strictly limit how many students got into the restaurant, and quell
40   any rowdiness before it got out of hand. I manned the front door, and stopped letting people in by
41   8:30, when we were as packed as we could safely be. The game was supposed to start at 9:00 pm,
42   and I took some heat from students who wanted in. I told the students who wanted to step outside
43   that once they were gone, they were gone. I know they thought I was a jerk, but it helped keep things
44   under control.
45
46   The crowd was in a good, excited mood, but got rowdier by the second half of the game. I
47   started seeing students standing on chairs to cheer and getting really worked up, so I put an end to

1 the beer sales by 10:30. I handled the complaints, because the wait staff had enough to do without
2 dealing with angry students, plus students were less likely to get out of control with me. I had to
3 escort one or two guys out, and then things stayed under control. I did not really follow the game,
4 although it seemed close. As the game was nearing the end, around 11:20 or so, I got a call from the
5 other Pizza Pub saying that they were having serious problems with some of the students there, as
6 a fight had started and a table or two had been pushed over. I told them to stop selling beer, and I
7 would come over as soon as the game was over. I realized I should have told them earlier to stop
8 selling beer. As I hung up the phone, I heard some shouting and saw students flocking to the front
9 door to leave. I helped Joe for a minute or two at the door making sure everyone got out, and then
10 realized that I would need to move my car if I was going to get to the other side of campus to help
11 at the other restaurant.
12
13 I got into my car, a white Miata, and pulled into Franklin Street. I saw that East Franklin was
14 already barricaded, and headed west to cut through Church Street onto Rosemary, so I could head
15 east. West Franklin was still pretty empty, although kids were starting to come out onto the street.
16 I drove up West Franklin, going no faster than the speed limit, which is 25. The rain was starting
17 to come down hard, and I had my wipers on. I had to open my side window a bit when the inside
18 of the windshield fogged up, so I could hear all the shouting and screaming that was going on.
19
20 I turned right on Church, and had to slow down. I couldn't have been going more than 15
21 m.p.h., maybe slower. By then there seemed to be kids everywhere; shouting and banging on my
22 car as they crossed the street. It wasn't as bad on Church as the news video showed it was on
23 Franklin, but it was still pretty wild. There were groups of kids on the sidewalks, and some on the
24 curb. Some kids were crossing west to east, and I had to slow down more. I heard a loud bang on
25 my trunk, and I turned my head to see what happened as I put on my brakes. I couldn't see who had
26 hit my car, and by the time I turned back around I could see that Church Street was getting crowded.
27
28 I stopped my car and stepped out far enough to see that there were groups of kids coming
29 from the Burger and Brew and the apartments at the far end of Church, and realized I could not make
30 it through safely. Kids were jumping around, shouting "We're Number 1" and generally acting as
31 you would expect. I saw some kids in front of my car, but I did not notice anyone on the ground.
32 I yelled at them to get out of the street and then I got back into my car, backed up a few feet, and
33 turned left into a parking lot, finding a spot near the back that was far enough away from the street
34 so that it would not be near where the kids were walking. I had heard horror stories of cars being
35 turned over the last time U.N.C. won a championship, and I wanted my car to be out of the way.
36
37 I used my car phone to call the other Pizza Pub, and they seemed to be getting things under
38 control. The telephone bill for my cellular phone indicates that this call was made at 11:29 p.m. and
39 lasted four minutes. After this call, I walked down some steps to Franklin Street, and then went to
40 the restaurant. I did not notice any ambulance, flashing lights or anything like that. It was raining,
41 and I was walking fast as I did not have an umbrella. I noticed police, but did not think that was
42 unusual. I went back to the Pizza Pub and helped Joe finish getting the kids out and lockup. While
43 Joe and the others cleaned up, I called the police station to report that my car might have been
44 damaged by the students. I called twice, but could not get through. I then called 911, but they told
45 me it was not an emergency and not to bother them. Sometime around midnight the crowds on West
46 Franklin seemed to have thinned, so I walked back to my car and drove home.
47

1   The next morning I drove to the airport to catch a plane to Kansas City. When I parked my
2   car I noticed a couple of dents in the car I had not noticed before, including one on the hood and one
3   near the back. I bought the car used, but I think I would have noticed those dents if they had been
4   there earlier. I do not know how the dent on my hood got there.
5
6   I was in Kansas City until Thursday night, when I flew back. I worked my normal schedule
7   from Friday until the day I was arrested. I do not remember anything unusual about my work habits
8   during this time period. I work twelve-fourteen hour days, and do not read the local paper or watch
9   the local news. I usually read *USA Today*. None of my employees mentioned anything to me, except
10   that Joe Cheshire may have mentioned that the police came by a day or two before my arrest. I did
11   not think much about it.
12
13   I was surprised and upset by my arrest. I did not think I had done anything wrong. I made
14   a statement to the police, although they told me I could talk to a lawyer first. I have spent a great
15   deal of my time working with young people, and I am angry anyone would think I would leave a
16   young person hurt in the road. Needless to say, this ruined my chance for the promotion. One of the
17   other candidates got the job. I am lucky I kept my job as district manager.

This deposition was taken in the office of plaintiff's counsel under oath on January 30, YR-1.

I have read the foregoing transcript of my deposition given on the date above and find it is
a true and accurate representation of my testimony.

Signed this _30_ day of ___January___ YR-_1_ at Nita City, Nita.

James Wyatt
JAMES WYATT, Deponent

Certified by:

Roger Davis
ROGER DAVIS
Certified Shorthand Reporter, (CSR)

JOE CHESHIRE

Deposition[*]

January 31, YR-1

1   Joe Cheshire, having being called to testify and being duly sworn, testifies as follows:
2

3   My name is Joe Cheshire and I live in Apartment 3, 1301 North Greensboro Street, which
4   is on the west side of Nita City. I am 24 years old, and I work for Business Machines Incorporated,
5   where I am a salesman. I graduated from U.N.C. in May of YR-2, with a degree in business and
6   computer science. It took me five years to finish college because I had to work while I was a student.
7   I worked at Pizza Pub, on Franklin Street, near the campus. I started out as a waiter, and then
8   became a cook in YR-3. In the fall of YR-3 I was promoted to manager by Mr. Wyatt, several
9   months after Mr. Wyatt became the District Manager.
10

11   Mr. Wyatt is a nice guy. He reminds me of my old high school football coach. He is hard
12   on you if he thinks you are not working, but treats you great if you are carrying your weight. In fact,
13   he fired the former manager because he was not taking the job seriously enough. Mr. Wyatt is all
14   business, and some of the staff did not like him because he had no patience for students who did not
15   focus on their jobs. I have never had problems with Mr. Wyatt, and he was pretty cool about my
16   schedule while I was in school as long as I worked hard when I was there.
17

18   I understand that Mr. Wyatt has been charged with being involved in an accident on the night
19   of April 5, YR-2. I remember that night because it was the night U.N.C. won the national
20   championship, and it was pretty wild. Mr. Wyatt had come by the restaurant during several of the
21   games U.N.C. played in the tournament, and seemed concerned that we keep things under control.
22   He would tell me that making money from the beer sales for one night was not worth it if the
23   restaurant got trashed. He was pretty strict about keeping the restaurant in good shape, and keeping
24   things under control. He mentioned to me that he expected to be promoted to Regional Manager,
25   and wanted to do good job running the stores while he was District Manager.
26

27   On April 5, YR-2, Mr. Wyatt came by the store before the championship game began,
28   probably by 7 p.m. Students had already started staking out tables to watch the game, and drinking
29   beer. Wyatt met with us, and told us to be very careful that things did not get out of control; he
30   warned us about collecting money for the food and beer before the game was over, and not letting
31   students get so drunk they would trash the store. He said he had tried to get some off-duty cops to
32   help out, but none were available. He said he had heard stories about the chaos that last time U.N.C.
33   won the national championship, and was not going to let anything happen to the restaurant this time.
34

35   I did not see Mr. Wyatt too much during the game; we were very busy, and he spent most of
36   the evening at the front door keeping students out once we were full. The place was packed, and the

---

[*]Cheshire was deposed in connection with a civil suit filed by Gilbert. The transcript of Cheshire's
testimony has been excerpted so that only the answers are reprinted here. Assume that he was called to testify by the
plaintiff, and that this is a true and accurate reproduction of his answers.

1 noise was deafening. The game was close, and everybody was shouting and screaming, having a
2 great time. At some point Mr. Wyatt told us to cut off the beer, and he went around and dealt with
3 the customers who got angry. Near the end of the game, Mr. Wyatt got a telephone call from the
4 other restaurant and then said he had to leave.

6 　　　He left in his white Miata, which he almost always parked in front of the restaurant. I was
7 at the front door dealing with getting folks out of the restaurant. Students were streaming down the
8 sidewalk toward East Franklin, and you could tell from the noise that the party had already started.
9 Mr. Wyatt seemed to be having a hard time getting on to Franklin Street. I saw him carefully nose
10 the car through the crowd on the sidewalk, sounding his horn, and then heard him drive off. I could
11 tell from the sound of the engine that he was not accelerating very fast as I did not hear him shift
12 gears. Mr Wyatt has driven me to the monthly managers meeting at the Estes Drive Pizza Pub, on
13 the other side of campus, several times, and he has always driven carefully and no faster than the
14 speed limit.

16 　　　I left with the night deposit bag right after Mr. Wyatt left. I took the bag to the bank around
17 the corner on West Rosemary, and what was normally a two to three minute walk took ten minutes.
18 It was raining lightly, and the street was a mad house of screaming, drunk students. There were
19 bonfires and kids climbing trees, and jumping on the one or two cars left on the street. I have seen
20 a videotape that Mr. Wyatt's lawyer got from the T.V. station, and it shows what was happening.
21 I was a bit nervous about carrying that much cash, but nobody seemed to pay any attention to me,
22 they were all too busy celebrating and screaming. When I got back, I noticed that Mr. Wyatt had
23 returned and was on the phone. I do not know when he returned. He seemed agitated about
24 something, but I could not really hear what he was saying. I was surprised he had come back to
25 make a call as he has a car phone. After he hung up, he slumped in one of the chairs and stared out
26 of the window. I asked, in a joking way, if he had run into a brick wall of students. He seemed a
27 little taken aback, sort of surprised, looked at me for a minute, and then said he had some type of
28 problem on Church Street with his car. He said some kids had jumped on the hood or trunk, and he
29 was waiting for the crowd to thin out. He did not look nervous, he just looked tired. Sometime
30 around midnight he left. I remember the time, because that's when I usually leave, but I had to stay
31 later that night to finish cleaning up. He mentioned that he would not be around for a few days, and
32 that he hoped to come back as Regional Manager.

34 　　　I left close to 1 a.m. I walked home. It was still raining, and I could still hear the party going
35 on on East Franklin Street, although West Franklin Street was pretty clear. I did not hear anything
36 about the accident until I read about it in the paper the next day. The accident got a lot of coverage
37 in the local papers and on T.V., and at work, where we get the *Nita Morning Globe*. Folks at the
38 Pizza Pub talked about it. One of the waitresses said she saw a description of the suspect, and she
39 joked that it sounded like Mr. Wyatt. She said she saw the "wanted poster" when the police came
40 to post it at the restaurant. We have a policy of not allowing flyers in our windows because, in a
41 college town, once you allow some flyers the whole window gets covered. I never saw the flyer, and
42 someone must have taken it down. I did see a description of the suspect in the newspaper, and it
43 kind of sounded like Mr. Wyatt, but could have been someone else. I never mentioned it to Mr.
44 Wyatt later because I never figured that he had been involved in the accident.

46 　　　I did not see Mr. Wyatt for the rest of that week. He came by a couple of times after he came
47 back from Kansas City and before his arrest, but not as often as before. He mentioned that our store

1　was running pretty well, and he needed to spend more time at the other stores. I did not notice his
2　car in front of the store when he was there, but the small driveway in front of our store is often filled.
3
4　　　　I spoke with a detective about this case a day or two before Mr. Wyatt was arrested. I was
5　working at the restaurant when he came by and introduced himself. I was a bit nervous about talking
6　to him about my boss, but I told him what I knew in response to his questions. He seemed mainly
7　to be interested in finding Mr. Wyatt, and asked me not to tell Mr Wyatt about his visit. The next
8　day I saw Mr. Wyatt when he came by the restaurant, and I mentioned to him that the detective had
9　come by. I figured Wyatt was entitled to know, and I felt disloyal not telling him. He asked what
10　the detective had wanted, but did not seem overly upset or surprised.

　　　　This deposition was taken in the office of plaintiff's counsel under oath on January 31, YR-1.

　　　　I have read the foregoing transcript of my deposition given on the date above and find it is
a true and accurate representation of my testimony.

　　　　Signed this 31 day of _January_ YR-1 at Nita City, Nita.

　　　　　　　　　　　_Joe Cheshire_____
　　　　　　　　　　　JOE CHESHIRE, Deponent

　　　　　　　　　　　Certified by:

　　　　　　　　　　　_Roger Davis_____
　　　　　　　　　　　ROGER DAVIS
　　　　　　　　　　　Certified Shorthand Reporter, (CSR)

PIZZA PUB, INC

123 MAIN STREET
KANSAS CITY, MO
816-555-8333
FAX: 816-555-8383

Detective Paul Burns
Nita City Police Department
Nita City, Nita

February 26, YR-1

VIA FAX

Dear Detective Burns:

As I told you during our recent telephone conversation, I am Vice President of Pizza Pub, Inc. Pizza Pub has its corporate offices in Kansas City. We own Pizza Pub restaurants throughout the country, and also grant franchises to independent operators of Pizza Pubs. I have been in my current position for five years. I previously was in charge of risk management for Pizza Pub, and was responsible for formulating and implementing policies concerning the safe operation of the restaurants, and dealing with claims made against the company. Since my promotion to Vice President, I have been responsible for overseeing the operations of the company owned restaurants, and meet regularly with Regional Managers, District Managers, and others involved in the day to day operation of the stores.

I know Mr. Wyatt through his association with the company. I have met with him frequently, and I am familiar with his background and his work evaluations. He came to us in YR-4 with a background in food service management, and we were impressed by his professional manner. He was hired as manager of a single restaurant in Evanston, Illinois, but was quickly promoted to District Manager for one of our districts in Nita, managing four stores. We fully expected him to rise to Regional Manager, and I let him know in YR-2 that I had my eye on him as a prime candidate for such a position, which was opening in May, YR-2. Promotion to Regional Manager would have involved a substantial increase in responsibilities, and in compensation. Up until his arrest, Mr. Wyatt appeared to be exceeding our expectations. He turned some marginally profitably restaurants into good performers, both by boosting business and by reducing losses due to theft etc. He worked very hard, and never made excuses for the problems his restaurants had early on, but rather honestly explained the problems to us and set out to fix them. He had always exhibited a great deal of interest in the students who are our customers and employees. In my opinion, he is a very truthful, gentle and caring person, and I can't imagine him doing what he is accused of. I know many other people here who know Mr. Wyatt share my feelings.

Due to the high quality of Mr. Wyatt's work, I had asked him to make a presentation at our first YR-2 quarterly review meeting in Kansas City. He had attended several management meetings, and I wanted to see how he would perform under the pressure of making a presentation. He was expected to present an evaluation of our new "Carnivores' Pizza" campaign.

When we spoke yesterday, I did not have a clear memory of the details of this meeting. My secretary pulled the files, and I have reviewed them. I now remember that the meeting was on April 7, YR-2, beginning at 9:00 a.m. We scheduled this meeting well in advance, and sent out memos to all of the people who were to attend. Mr. Wyatt flew in the day before, as did most of the people attending the meeting. I have enclosed copies of the memos sent to everyone, and a list of the airline reservations that my secretary made.

Mr. Wyatt was at the meeting, and made his presentation, which went well. I spoke to him briefly at the meeting to tell him that I had been impressed, and made arrangements to eat breakfast with him the next morning. We met for breakfast on April 8, with several other people from the company. I do not remember all the specifics, but there was some general small talk, including some talk about U.N.C.'s recent victory in the NCAA tournament. I am a bit of a basketball fan, and Mr. Wyatt and I spoke about the game. He said he had not been able to see most of it because he was busy keeping things under control at the restaurant, but he did see "Little Pearl" Williams hit the three pointer that won the game. He also explained that the town was a zoo once the kids started celebrating, and mentioned that some kids had jumped on his car, or hit it with something, while he was driving from one restaurant to the other, and asked whether company insurance would cover damage to his car in such an incident. I explained that we expected our managers to carry sufficient insurance on their cars, and he let the matter drop. Mr. Wyatt flew back to Nita on an afternoon flight on the 8th of April, YR-2.

Mr. Wyatt called as soon as he was arrested, and told us that the matter would be taken care of. He said he had not hit anybody, and that this must be a case of mistaken identity as all of the witnesses were drunk college students. Based upon our assessment of Mr. Wyatt's character, we believe what he said. We support James, but we did not feel we could promote him while the case was pending. We therefore gave the Regional Manager position that came open to Sally Brown. However, this in no way reflects adversely on Mr. Wyatt. When this matter is resolved favorably to Mr. Wyatt, as we fully expect, he will be considered for the next Regional Manger position.

Sincerely,
dictated and signed for

Wade Smith

MEMORANDUM

TO: **Area Vice Presidents**
             Regional Managers
             District Managers

FROM: **Wade Smith**

DATE: **March 9, YR-2**

RE: **1st Quarter Business Review Meeting**

The 1st Quarter Business Review Meeting will be held on April 7 and 8 at the Kansas City Hyatt (formerly the Hilton East) in Kansas City.

Susan is working with Cathy at American Express Travel on flight arrangements. You should plan on arriving in Kansas City on Tuesday evening, April 6, and you may return to your districts late afternoon on Thursday, April 8. Tickets will be forwarded to you as soon as arrangements have been made.

If you should have any questions regarding our Business Review Meeting, don't hesitate to contact me.

Wade
JD/sh

True copy made this 26th day of February, YR-1.

Wade Smith
_____
Wade Smith

MEMORANDUM

TO: **Area Vice Presidents**
                Regional Managers
                District Managers

FROM: **Susan Harris**

DATE: **April 1, YR-2**

<u>**RE:**   **1st Quarter Business Review Meeting**</u>

Enclosed you will find your airline ticket for the Business Review meeting in Kansas City next week.

I have arranged for the hotel's van to pick some of you up upon arrival (the van only holds nine or ten people). The hotel has been given a schedule of your arrival times and your names, and the van will be waiting for you at the baggage terminal entrance to the airport. A few of you will have to call a cab when you arrive in Kansas City. Attached is a copy of the arrival schedule for your convenience.

I am also enclosing a rooming list. If you have any questions regarding the Kansas City meeting, don't hesitate to let me know.

Looking forward to seeing you again.

/sh

Enclosures

cc: Wade Smith

True copy made this 26th day of February, YR-1.

Wade Smith
_____
Wade Smith

ARRIVALS-TUESDAY, APRIL 6

Name	Arrival Time	Flight	Van/Other
Howard Walter	4:10 p.m.	Delta 960	Van
Ron Corder	4:17 p.m.	NW825	Van
Kathy Mitchell	4:17 p.m.	NW825	Van
Ed Wright	4:17 p.m.	NW825	Van
Ed Rogosich	4:52 p.m.	TWA 695	Van
Marc Cardillo	4:52 p.m.	TWA 695	Van
George Konawicz	4:52 p.m.	TWA 695	Van
Stewart McAdams	4:52 p.m.	TWA 695	Van
Mark Reynolds	4:52 p.m.	TWA 695	Van
Jeff Steinert	4:52 p.m.	TWA 695	Van
James Wyatt	4:59 p.m.	American 619	Cab
Brian Toutloff	4:59 p.m.	American 619	Cab
Bill Weniger	4:59 p.m.	American 619	Cab
Don Pollan	4:59 p.m.	American 619	Cab
Bob Magolnick	7:15 p.m.	USAIR 5625	Van
John Forster	7:15 p.m.	USAIR 5625	Van
Ernie Connatser	7:15 p.m.	USAIR 5625	Van
Lenny Furman	8:15 p.m.	Delta 743	Van
Jim Raynor	8:41 p.m.	United 553	Van
John Whittington	8:41 p.m.	United 553	Van
Bob Hoover	8:41 p.m.	United 553	Van

DEPARTURES-THURSDAY, APRIL 8

Name	Departure Time	Flight	Van/Other
Ed Rogosich	2:35 p.m.	United 1498	Van
Marc Cardillo	2:35 p.m.	United 1498	Van
Buddy Wilkins	2:35 p.m.	United 1498	Van
John Whittington	2:35 p.m.	United 1498	Van
George Konawicz	2:35 p.m.	United 1498	Van
Stewart McAdams	2:35 p.m.	United 1498	Van
Mark Reynolds	2:57 p.m.	TWA 138	Van
Jeff Steinert	2:57 p.m.	TWA 138	Van
Ernie Connatser	3:17 p.m.	American 740	Other
Jim Raynor	3:17 p.m.	American 740	Other
James Wyatt	3:17 p.m.	American 740	Other
Lenny Furman	3:17 p.m.	American 740	Other
Bob Magolnick	3:17 p.m.	American 740	Other
John Forster	3:17 p.m.	American 740	Other
Don Pollan	3:17 p.m.	American 740	Other
Bob Hoover	3:17 p.m.	American 740	Other
Brian Toutloff	3:25 p.m.	US Air 5616	Other
Bill Weniger	3:25 p.m.	US Air 5616	Other
Howard Walter	3:25 p.m.	US Air 5616	Other
Ron Corder	5:20 p.m.	NW 826	Van
Ed Wright	6:30 p.m.	Delta 608	Van
Kathy Mitchell	6:30 p.m.	Delta 608	Van

CRIMINAL CASE

PROPOSED JURY INSTRUCTIONS

1.   The Court will now instruct you on the law governing this case. You must arrive at your verdict by unanimous vote, applying the law, as you are now instructed, to the facts as you find them to be.

2.   The State of Nita has charged the Defendant, James Wyatt, with the crimes of Reckless Driving and Hit and Run with Personal Injury. The Defendant has pleaded not guilty.

3.   Under the criminal code of the State of Nita, a person commits the crime of reckless driving if he drives a vehicle on any street or highway without due caution and circumspection and at a speed or in a manner so as to endanger or be likely to endanger any person or property.

4.   Thus, to sustain the charge of reckless driving, the State must prove three things beyond a reasonable doubt:

First, that the Defendant drove a vehicle upon a public highway. Church Street in Nita City is a public highway.

Second, that he drove that vehicle without due caution or circumspection.

And Third, that he drove at a speed or in a manner so as to endanger or be likely to endanger any person or property.

So I charge that if you find from the evidence beyond a reasonable doubt that on or about April 5, YR-2, James Wyatt drove a vehicle upon Church Street, and that in so doing he acted without due caution or circumspection and at a speed or in a manner so as to endanger or be likely to endanger any person or property, it would be your duty to return a verdict of guilty as charged. However, if you do not so find or if you have a reasonable doubt as to one or more of these things, it would be your duty to return a verdict of not guilty.

5.   Under the criminal code of the State of Nita, a person commits the crime of Hit and Run with Personal Injury if he knows or reasonably should know that the vehicle he is operating is involved in an accident that has resulted in injury to any person, and does not immediately stop his vehicle and remain at the scene until a law enforcement officer authorizes him to leave.

6.   Thus, to sustain the charge of Hit and Run with Physical Injury, the State must prove six things beyond a reasonable doubt:

First, that the Defendant was driving the vehicle.

Second, that the vehicle was involved in an accident.

Third, that someone was physically injured in this accident. A broken leg and a closed head injury constitute "physical injury" under the statute.

Fourth, that the Defendant knew or reasonably should have known that he had struck a pedestrian and that the pedestrian suffered physical injury in the accident. The Defendant's knowledge can be actual or implied--that is, it can be inferred where the circumstances are such as would lead a driver to believe that he had been in an accident which caused physical injury to a person.

Fifth, that the Defendant, after stopping, did not remain at the scene of the accident until a law enforcement officer authorized him to leave.

And Sixth, that the Defendant's failure to remain was willful, that is, intentional and without justification or excuse.

So I charge that if you find from the evidence beyond a reasonable doubt that on or about April 5, YR-2, the Defendant was driving a vehicle that was involved in an accident in which a person was physically injured, and that the Defendant knew or reasonably should have known that someone had been physically injured and failed to remain until he was authorized to leave, and that the Defendant's failure to remain was intentional and without justification or excuse, it would be your duty to return a verdict of guilty of hit and run with personal injury. However, if you do not so find, or if you have a reasonable doubt as to one or more of these things, it would be your duty to return a verdict of not guilty of hit and run with personal injury.

7.   Flight. The State contends that the Defendant fled from the scene of the accident. Evidence of flight may be considered by you, together with all other facts and circumstances in this case, in determining whether the combined circumstances amount to an admission or show consciousness of guilt of the offense of reckless driving. However, proof of this circumstance is not sufficient, in itself, to establish Defendant's guilt of the offense of reckless driving.

NITA STATUTES

CH 20. MOTOR VEHICLES

§20-140. Reckless driving.

(a) Any person who drives any vehicle upon a highway or any public vehicular area without due caution and circumspection and at a speed or in a manner so as to endanger or be likely to endanger any person or property shall be guilty of reckless driving.

(b) Reckless driving as defined in subsection (a) is a misdemeanor, punishable by imprisonment not to exceed six months or a fine not to exceed five hundred dollars ($500.00), or both a fine and imprisonment.

§20-166. Hit and run.

(a) The driver of any vehicle who knows or reasonably should know:

(1) That the vehicle which he is operating is involved in an accident or collision; and

(2) That the accident or collision has resulted in injury or death to any person; shall immediately stop his vehicle at the scene of the accident or collision. He shall remain at the scene of the accident until a law-enforcement officer completes his investigation of the accident or collision or authorizes him to leave; Provided, however, that he may leave to call for a law-enforcement officer or for medical assistance or medical treatment as set forth in (b), but must return to the accident scene within a reasonable period of time. A willful violation of this subsection shall be punished as a Class I felony.

(b) the driver of any vehicle, when he knows or reasonably should know that the vehicle which he is operating is involved in an accident or collision, which accident or collision results only in damage to property shall immediately stop his vehicle at the scene of the accident or collision. A violation of this subsection is a misdemeanor punishable by a fine or by imprisonment for not more than two years, or both, in the discretion of the court.

§20-174. Crossing at other than crosswalks; walking along highway.

(a) Every pedestrian crossing a roadway at any point other than within a marked crosswalk or within an unmarked crosswalk at an intersection shall yield the right-of-way to all vehicles upon the roadway.

(b) Between adjacent intersections at which traffic-control signals are in operation pedestrians shall not cross at any place except in a marked crosswalk.

(c) Where sidewalks are provided, it shall be unlawful for any pedestrian to walk along and upon an adjacent roadway. Where sidewalks are not provided, any pedestrian walking along and upon a highway shall, when practicable, walk only on the extreme left of the roadway or its shoulder facing traffic which may approach from the opposite direction. Such pedestrian shall yield the right-of-way to approaching traffic.

(d) Notwithstanding the provisions of this section, every driver of a vehicle shall exercise due care to avoid colliding with any pedestrian upon any roadway, and shall give warning by sounding the horn when necessary, and shall exercise proper precaution upon observing any child or any confused or incapacitated person upon a roadway.

State v. Wyatt

IN THE CIRCUIT COURT OF
DARROW COUNTY, NITA

THE STATE OF NITA,	)	
	)	
	)	
vs.	)	**JURY VERDICT**
	)	
JAMES WYATT,	)	
	)	
Defendant.	)	
	)	

We, the Jury, return the following verdict, and each of us concurs in this verdict:

[Choose the appropriate verdict]

I. <u>RECKLESS DRIVING</u>

We, the Jury, find the Defendant, James Wyatt, NOT GUILTY of Reckless Driving.

_____

FOREPERSON

We, the Jury, find the Defendant, James Wyatt, GUILTY of Reckless Driving.

_____

FOREPERSON

II. <u>HIT AND RUN WITH PERSONAL INJURY</u>

We, the Jury, find the Defendant, James Wyatt, NOT GUILTY of Hit and Run with Personal Injury.

_____

FOREPERSON

We, the Jury, find the Defendant, James Wyatt, GUILTY of Hit and Run with Personal Injury.

_____

FOREPERSON